TRAINING CURRICULUM

JOHN C. MAXWELL

LEADERSHIP GOLD

LESSONS I'VE LEARNED *from a* LIFETIME *of* LEADING

PARTICIPANT GUIDE

Table of Contents

LEADERSHIP GOLD

LETTER *from* JOHN C. MAXWELL

Dear Friend:

You are about to embark on a personal growth journey based upon the content in my book *Leadership Gold*. I confess I've wanted to write this book for almost a decade, but I promised myself I wouldn't do it until I turned sixty. In February of 2007 I reached that milestone and started writing.

My desire was to put the hardest-won leadership lessons of my life into a book that could be used to mentor leaders. I've sifted through a lot of dirt in order to deliver the gold.

Leadership Gold is my most personal work yet. It is filled with stories of my leadership failures and successes and the nuggets of wisdom I have gained as a result.

I am delighted that my my friends at The John Maxwell Company used *Leadership Gold* to develop this training kit. I had fun teaching it and I hope you have fun watching it.

If you are an emerging leader you will love the foundation this training kit provides. Experienced leaders will enjoy the insights and examples and will want to use the materials to develop the next generation of leaders on their team.

Remember, good leadership always makes a difference! I've seen it turn around organizations and positively impact the lives of thousands of individuals. Turn the page and let's start learning.

Your friend,

John C. Maxwell

INTRODUCTION

This book is designed to emphasize what you should learn from the DVDs. Take pertinent notes while you watch them and use the following three codes to highlight key points you will ACT on:

> Put an "**A**" next to the lessons you want to learn to **A**pply in your life
>
> Put a "**C**" next to the lessons you need to **C**hange, lessons you've been applying wrong
>
> Put a "**T**" next to lessons you want to **T**ransfer to someone else

To then make the most of the lessons, spend two weeks with each of the twenty-six lessons in the following manner:

1. Spend the first week modeling the lesson yourself
2. Spend the second week teaching it to someone you are leading

By following this model, you and those around you will benefit from the lessons of *Leadership Gold* for an entire year.

After you have completed your journey, continue to use your notes as a handy reference for your ongoing leadership development and the development of those you will lead in the future.

LESSON 1:

If It's Lonely at the Top, You're Not Doing Something ___________

My father's generation believed that leaders should never get too close to the people they lead. "Keep a distance" was a phrase I often heard. Good leaders were supposed to be a little above and apart from followers. As a result, when I began my leadership journey, I made sure to keep some distance between me and the people I was leading. I tried to be close enough to lead them but far enough away to not be influenced by them. I eventually learned that:

Loneliness is not a _________________ issue.

> *Cartoon: An executive is shown sitting forlornly behind a huge desk. Standing meekly on the other side of the desk is a man dressed in work clothes, who says, "If it's any comfort to you, it's lonely at the bottom too."*

Being at the top doesn't mean you have to be lonely. Neither does being at the bottom. I've met lonely people at the bottom, on the top, and in the middle. My conclusion:

Loneliness is not a ________________ issue; it's a ________________ issue.

If you're lonely, it's not because you have a particular title or position. Your personality is the culprit.

Advice to Lonely Leaders

- Avoid ______________ ______________

  Leadership is as much relational as it is positional. An individual who takes a relational approach to leadership will never be lonely.

- Realize the ________________ of Success and Failure

  Success can be dangerous—and so can failure. Think of yourself as "a success" and you start to separate yourself from those you view as less successful. You start to think, *I don't need to see them*, and you withdraw. Ironically, failure also leads to withdrawal. Think of yourself as "a failure" and you avoid others, thinking, *I don't want to see them.* Both extremes in thinking can create an unhealthy separation from others.

I've gone from:

"It's lonely at the top"

to

"If it's lonely at the top, I'm doing something wrong"

to

"Come up to the top and join me"

to

"Let's go to the top together"

to

"It's not lonely at the top."

LESSON 2:

The Toughest Person to Lead Is Always ______________

Acknowledging that leading myself is a challenge brings back some painful memories. Many of my leadership breakdowns have been personal breakdowns. In a leadership career that has spanned almost four decades, I've made plenty of mistakes but I have experienced only four major leadership crises. Unfortunately, all of them were my fault.

If I could kick the person responsible for my leadership problems, I wouldn't be able to sit down for a week.

The power of leadership is in your ability to do it first.

Keys To Leading Yourself

- Learn ______________

  "Civilization is always in danger when those who have never learned to obey are given the right to command."

  --Bishop Fulton J. Sheen

  Only a leader who has followed well knows how to lead others well. Leaders who have not followed well, tend to be:

  (1) ______________ (3) ______________

  (2) ______________ (4) ______________

- Seek Accountability

  People who lead themselves well know a secret: they can't ______________ ______________. Good leaders know that power can be seductive, and they understand their own fallibility. To be a leader and deny this is to put yourself in danger.

"When you see a good man, think of _______________ him;

When you see a bad man, _______________ your heart."

--Chinese Proverb

> *When Harry Truman was thrust into the presidency upon the death of Franklin Roosevelt, Sam Rayburn gave him some fatherly advice: "From here on out you're going to have lots of people around you. They'll try to put a wall around you and cut you off from any ideas but theirs. They'll tell you what a great man you are, Harry. But you and I both know you ain't."*

Thomas J. Watson, the former chairman of IBM, said, "Nothing so conclusively proves a man's ability to lead others as what he does from day to day to lead himself." How true.

The smallest crowd you will ever lead is you—but it's the most important one. Do that well and you earn the right to lead bigger crowds.

NOTES

LESSON 3:

Defining __________ Define Your __________

One of the leaders I admire most is Winston Churchill, the prime minister of England who stood against the Nazis during World War II. He was a leader's leader who once remarked, "In every age there comes a time when a leader must come forward to meet the needs of the hour. Therefore, there is no potential leader who does not have an opportunity to make a positive difference in society. Tragically, there are times when a leader does not rise to the hour."

The key question: What will determine whether *you* will step forward to successfully meet the challenges you face? I believe the determining factor is how you handle certain critical moments in your life. These moments define who you are as a person and as a leader.

Moments That Defined Me

- *Some defining moments were __________ breakers ...*

  They took me into an area I hadn't been before.

- *Some defining moments were __________ breakers ...*

  They were moments when I realized things were not going well.

During this season, I learned a lesson that is best described by Brian Dyson, former vice chairman and COO of Coca-Cola:

Imagine life as a game in which you are juggling some five balls in the air. You name them—work, family, health, friends and spirit—and you're keeping all of these in the air. You will soon understand that work is a rubber ball. If you drop it, it will bounce back. But the other four balls—family, health, friends and spirit are made of glass. If you drop one of these, they will be irrevocably scuffed, marked, nicked, damaged or even shattered. They will never be the same. You must understand that and strive for balance in your life.

- *Some defining moments were ____________ breakers …*

  They let me soar like I'd never soared before

- *Some defining moments were ____________ breakers …*

  They took me beyond my expectations

At every defining moment, you must ask one question:

What did I learn?

Experience is no teacher unless you learn from it. Focus not on what happens to you but on what happens in you during the process of the experience.

NOTES

LESSON 4:

When You Get Kicked in the Rear, You Know You're Out in ________

One of the prices of leadership is criticism. When spectators watch a race, where do they focus their attention? On the frontrunners. Few people pay close attention to the racers who are out of contention.

> *When you're getting discouraged as a leader, think of Moses. He led a million complaining people for forty years and never arrived where he was supposed to go. Moses faced a lot of complaints, criticism, and just plain whining. Some days as a leader, I can sympathize with Moses. I bet if he had it to do all over again, he would have made a note to self: Next time don't tell Pharaoh to let all my people go.*

How to Hold Up Under Criticism

Greek philosopher Aristotle said, "Criticism is something you can avoid easily—by saying nothing, doing nothing and being nothing." However, that isn't an option for anyone who wants to be a successful leader. So what do you do? The following four-step process has helped me deal with criticism, so I pass it on to you:

Step 1. __________ Yourself—This Is a ______________ Issue

Know what you do well.

I excel at…

- ______________________
- ______________________
- ______________________

Know what you don't do well.

I struggle at…

- ________________________
- ________________________
- ________________________

No leader is perfect and many times your weaknesses float to the top. You must know yourself well. If you don't, you'll never be able to help others with theirs. You cannot impart what you do not possess.

Step 2. _______________ Yourself —This Is a _______________ Issue

Leaders change first.

"You shall know the truth and the truth shall make you mad."
--Aldous Huxley

"Some people are like sea gulls. When something goes wrong, they fly in, make a lot of noise and crap all over everything."
--Ken Blanchard

People can change for the better only when they are open to improvement. For that reason, when I am criticized I try to maintain the right attitude by:

- Not being _____________
- Looking for the grain of _____________
- Making the necessary _____________
- Taking the __________ __________

Ultimately, there are only two kinds of criticism:

1. The kind that's unfair and not right

2. The kind that's right on target

You must know what to do with the second kind. Change what needs changing.

Step 3. ____________ Yourself—This Is a ____________ Issue

Professor and author Leo Buscaglia counseled, "The easiest thing to be in the world is you. The most difficult thing to be is what other people want you to be. Don't let them put you in that position."

To be the best person you can be—and the best leader—you need to be yourself. That doesn't mean that you aren't willing to grow and change. It just means that you work to become the best you that you can be. Then, as psychologist Carl Rogers remarked, "The curious paradox is that when I accept myself just as I am, then I can change." Being who you really are is the first step in becoming better than you are.

> *"Blessed are those who can laugh at themselves. They shall never cease to be entertained."*
>
> *--Chinese proverb*

The foundation of leadership development = accepting yourself.

Step 4. ____________ Yourself—This Is a ____________ Issue

The final step in the process of effectively handling criticism is to stop focusing on yourself. When we were growing up, a lot of us spent a good deal of time worrying about what the world thought of us. Now I'm sixty and I realize the world really wasn't paying much attention.

My policy: when entering a room, go to critics first. Tell them you value and appreciate them. Uncross their arms. Take the high road. We all need grace and forgiveness.

NOTES

LESSON 5:

Never _______ A Day In Your Life

Following your ______________ is the key to finding your ________________.

What does a leader need to succeed? Passion. Passion is a real difference-maker. It separates the extraordinary from the ordinary. When I think back on my career, I recognize that passion has enabled me to do the following:

- ____________ things I would not have believed.
- ____________ things I would not have felt.
- ____________ things I would not have attempted.
- ____________ things I would not have accomplished.
- ____________ people I would not have met.
- ____________ people I would not have motivated.
- ____________ people I would not have led.

"The world will belong to passionate, driven leaders… people who not only have enormous amounts of energy, but who can energize those whom they lead."

--Jack Welch

I have yet to meet an individual who reached his or her potential who didn't possess passion. **Tap into your passion and unlock the key to your potential.**

LESSON 6:

The Best Leaders Are ______________.

Steven Sample, in his book The Contrarian's Guide to Leadership writes, "The average person suffers from three delusions:

1. That he is a good driver

2. That he has a good sense of humor

3. That he is a good listener."

We can often hear what is said without listening to what is being communicated.

Why Listeners Make More Effective Leaders

- **Listening is the Best Way to ___________**

  It is no accident that we have one mouth and two ears. When we fail to listen we shut off half of our learning potential.

  "I remind myself every morning: Nothing I say this day will teach me anything. So, if I'm going to learn, I must do it by listening."

  --Larry King

- **Listening Can Keep Problems from ___________**

  "Listen to the whispers and you won't have to hear the screams."

  --Cherokee proverb

  The higher people go in leadership, the more authority they wield and the less they are forced to listen to others. However, their need to listen increase more than ever. The farther leaders get from the front lines, the more they must depend on others for accurate information.

Listening Can Improve the ___________

The bottom line: when the leader listens, the organization gets better.

"Listening can make the difference between a mediocre company and a great one."

-- Lee Iacocca

Leaders need to listen before they lead. Listen well and you'll lead well.

NOTES

LESSON 7:

Get in the Zone and __________ ______________

"Almost every man wastes part of his life in attempts to display qualities which he does not possess."

--Samuel Johnson

Finding Your Own Strength Zone

Step 1: Ask, "What am I Doing __________?"

People who reach their potential spend less time asking "What am I doing right?" and more time asking, "What am I doing well?" The first is a moral question; the second is a talent question. You should always strive to do what's right. But doing what's right doesn't tell you anything about your talent.

Step 2: _______ ____________.

When we consider our strengths, we tend to think too broadly.

"The great mystery isn't that people do things badly but that they occasionally do a few things well. The only thing that is universal is incompetence. Strength is always specific!"

--Peter Drucker

"Discover uniqueness, then discipline yourself to develop it."

--Jim Sundberg, Former all-star catcher

The Gallup organization conducted research on 1.7 million people in the workplace. According to their findings, only 20 percent of employees feel that their strengths are in play every day in the work setting. In my opinion, that is largely the fault of their leaders. They have failed to help their people find their strengths and place them in the organization where their strengths can be an asset to the company.

It's the leader's job to help people find their strengths. It is everyone's job to develop his or her unique strength. Ask yourself, "What is my unique strength that sets me apart from everyone else?"

NOTES

LESSON 8:

A Leader's First Responsibility Is to Define ____________

While trying to resolve an important issue in my company, I read a book called *Jack: Straight From the Gut* by Jack Welch. In it were the following six rules for successful leadership:

Rule #1: Control your destiny, or someone else will.

Rule #2: Face reality as it is, not as it was or as you wish it were.

Rule #3: Be candid with everyone.

Rule #4: Don't manage; lead.

Rule #5: Change before you have to.

Rule #6: If you don't have a competitive advantage, don't compete.

As I read this advice from the CEO of CEOs, I realized that five of his six rules for successful leadership were about facing reality. It was like having a bucket of cold water thrown in my face. When I returned home, I gathered my key people around me, read them the six rules, and announced the changes I would be making within the company.

The Law of the Scoreboard:

"The Team Can Make Adjustments When It Knows

__________ ______ __________."

For the next five years I kept Welch's six rules in my briefcase. I often pulled them out and re-read them, especially when I was facing yet another difficult leadership decision.

Bill Easum, president and senior managing partner in Easum, Bandy and Associates, asserts, "Realistic leaders are objective enough to minimize illusions. They understand that self-deception can cost them their vision."

If you are optimistic, as I am, and you naturally encourage people, as I do, then you may need to take extra care to look reality in the eye and keep yourself grounded. Continually cast a realistic eye on the following:

- The Situation – It is often ____________ than you think.
- The Process – It usually takes ____________ than you think.
- The Price – It always costs ____________ than you think.

NOTES

LESSON 9:

To See How the Leader Is Doing, ____________ at the ____________.

"The signs of outstanding leadership appear primarily among the followers."

--Max Depree

If you want to know how you're doing as a leader (or if you want to analyze the leadership of someone else in your organization), do it by asking the following four questions:

Question #1: Are the people ____________?

All leaders have two common characteristics: First, they are going somewhere; second, they are able to persuade other people to go with them. In a very practical sense, the second characteristic is what separates the real leaders from the pretenders. If someone with a leadership position has no followers, then that person has a position but isn't really a leader. There is no such thing as a leader without followers.

Question #2: Are the people ____________?

The second question has to do with whether the people are willing to make changes for the sake of progress. Progress does not occur without change.

"Men make history and not the other way around. In periods where there is no leadership society stands still. Progress occurs when courageous, skillful leaders seize the opportunity to change things for the better."

--President Harry S. Truman

Question #3: Are the people ____________?

"The growth and development of people is the highest calling of a leader."
--Dale Galloway

The best leaders help people with more than their jobs; they help them with their lives. They help them to become better people, not just better workers. They enlarge them. And that has great power because growing people create growing organizations.

Walter Bruckart, former vice president of Circuit City, noted that the top five factors of excellence in an organization are

1. people,
2. people,
3. people,
4. people, and
5. people.

As a leader, my success in developing others will depend upon my:

- High valuation of people – This is an ______________ issue.
- High commitment to people – This is a ______________ issue.
- High integrity with people – This is a ______________ issue.
- High standard for people – This is a ________________ issue.
- High influence over people – This is a ______________ issue.

Question #4: Are the people succeeding?

Leaders may ____________ others when they succeed, but they

______________ others when their followers succeed.

"Leadership is the lifting of a man's vision to higher sights, the raising of a man's performance to a higher standard, the building of a man's personality beyond its normal limitations."

--Peter Drucker

Leadership is meant to lift others.

NOTES

LESSON 10:

Don't Send Your Ducks to

____________ ____________.

Don't spin your wheels trying to turn ducks into eagles.

Three Reasons Not To Send Your Ducks to Eagle School

Reason #1:
If You Send Ducks to Eagle School, You Will Frustrate the __________

Leadership is all about placing people in the right place so they can be successful. As a leader, you need to know and value your people for who they are and let them work according to their strengths. There's nothing wrong with ducks. Just don't ask them to soar or hunt from a high altitude. It's not what they do.

Author, pastor and Dallas Theological Seminary chancellor Charles Swindoll illustrates this principle in his book, *Growing Strong in the Seasons of Life* when he writes,

> Once upon a time, the animals decided they should do something meaningful to meet the problems of the new world.
> So they organized a school.
>
> They adopted an activity curriculum of running, climbing, swimming, and flying. To make it easier to administer, all the animals took all the subjects.
>
> The duck was excellent in swimming. In fact, he was better than his instructor was! However, he made only passing grades in flying, and was very poor in running. Since he was so slow in running, he had to drop swimming and stay after school to practice running. This caused his webbed feet to be badly worn so he became only average in swimming. But "average" was quite acceptable, therefore nobody worried about it—except the duck.
>
> The rabbit started at the top of his class in running, but developed a nervous twitch in his leg muscles because he had so much makeup work to do in swimming.

> The squirrel was excellent in climbing, but he encountered constant frustration in flying class because his teacher made him start from the ground up instead of from the treetop down. He developed "charley horses" from overexertion, so he only got a "C" in climbing and a "D" in running.
>
> The eagle was a problem child and was severely disciplined for being a non-conformist. In climbing classes, he beat all the others to the top, but insisted on using his own way of getting there.

Reason #2:
If You Send Ducks to Eagle School, You Will Frustrate the ___________

My mother used to say, "Birds of a feather flock together." That's really true. Eagles don't want to hang around with ducks. They don't want to live in a barnyard or swim in a pond. Their potential makes them impatient with those who cannot soar.

Reason #3:
If You Send Ducks to Eagle School, You Will Frustrate _____________

Have you ever led people who never did rise up and fulfill your expectations? No matter how much you motivated them, trained them, provided them with resources or gave them opportunities, they just didn't perform according to your expectations. That's happened to me many times.

Maybe they weren't the problem. Maybe you were. A familiar Mother Goose rhyme reads:

> Pussy Cat, Pussy Cat, where have you been?
> I've been to London to visit the queen.
> Pussy Cat, Pussy Cat, what did you there?
> I frightened a little mouse under the chair.

Why did the cat start chasing a mouse in London when he was there to see the queen—a once in a lifetime opportunity? Because he was a cat. What else would you expect him to do?

Eagles are meant to soar. Ducks are meant to swim. Don't send your ducks to eagle school.

Picking Potential Leaders

John C. Maxwell

The Law of the Inner Circle: *Those who are closest to me will determine the level of my success.*

The year was 1864. The battle for America's future had been raging for over two and a half years. Brother fought brother and neighbor fought neighbor to determine the destiny of a nation.

Despite having a superior economy, an enormous edge in resources, and a far greater population, the North had been unable to gain the upper hand in the Civil War. President Abraham Lincoln was frustrated at the North's inability to achieve victory.

Lincoln was forced to confront the reality of the Law of the Inner Circle. Although a brilliant leader, Lincoln was not a military man. As such, his success overseeing the Civil War depended upon finding a skillful field general to translate material advantages into actual victories.

Lincoln's two prior military commanders, George McClellan and Henry Halleck, had failed miserably. Each had repeatedly squandered opportunities to crush the Southern Army. With the war's outcome hanging in the balance, Lincoln's next selection would be one of the biggest decisions of his Presidency.

Noting the indecisiveness of previous army generals, Lincoln chose tough-minded Ulysses S. Grant to lead the army. Grant's willingness to pay the price of a total war depleted the South's scant resources, and led to the North's eventual victory.

Identifying Potential Leaders

Good leaders realize the significance of surrounding themselves with talented people. That's why leaders repeatedly ask me, "How can I be sure to hire the right person?"

I have never discovered a foolproof hiring practice, but I do know finding a great hire goes hand in hand with identifying potential leaders.

I'd like to explore eleven questions I use to spot a potential leader. Before I begin, I'd like to give credit to my mentor and friend Fred Smith. Several of these questions were developed from my conversations with him.

1. When looking for a leader, do I see a constructive spirit of discontent?

Constructive discontent is a leader's unscratchable itch. It's the trait making a leader averse to average and opposed to the status quo.

Potential leaders possessing constructive discontent will question existing systems and push for improvements. They perceive problems and come up with solutions.

As Kouzes and Posner say, leaders have a pioneering instinct. They are not afraid to step out into the unknown. They are willing to take risks, innovate, and experiment in order to find new and better ways to operate.

2. Do they offer practical ideas?

Highly original thinkers can have problems leading when they are unable to judge their ideas realistically. Brainstorming is not a helpful practice in leadership unless useful ideas are generated.

In the words of John Galsworthy, "Idealism increases in direct proportion to one's distance from the problem." Potential leaders have the rare ability to translate idealistic goals into realistic and workable actions. Leaders are not frozen when obstacles disrupt the perfect plan. They have the flexibility and fortitude to account for resistance to the ideal.

3. When they speak, who listens?

Potential leaders have a "holding court" quality about them. Their words carry weight. What they say is valuable and inspires action.

When watching groups of people interact, in a matter of five minutes, I can pick the leader every time. When it comes time for the group to make a decision, all eyes focus upon the person with the greatest influence.

The extent of a person's influence speaks volumes about their potential in leadership. Here are seven key areas to evaluate the level of influence in a possible hire:

Character — who they are.

Relationships — who they know.

Knowledge — what they know.

Passion — how strongly they feel.

Experience — where they've been.

Past successes — what they've done.

Ability — what they can do.

4. Do others respect them?

Respect is vital for leadership, yet it can be difficult to discern in young leaders who have not fully developed. Peer respect doesn't reveal ability, but it shows character. I'll conclude this edition with the following acronym on respect. I have found it to be a helpful device to evaluate the respectability of emerging leaders.

R — Respects their coworkers and exhibits self-respect. Instead of asking for respect, they give it and earn it.

E — Exceeds the expectations of others. Naturally sets the bar higher than anybody else sets it for them.

S — Stands firm on convictions and values.

P — Possesses maturity well beyond their years and shows self-confidence.

E — Experiences a healthy family life.

C — Contributes to the success of others.

T — Thinks ahead of others. Potential leaders are marked by their ability to outpace the thinking of those around them.

5. Can they create or catch a vision?

I have a subset of four questions I try to answer when evaluating a potential leader's ability to catch or cast a vision:

Are they able to become a part of someone else's vision before they demand that others follow their vision?
I watch emerging leaders to see if they can catch a vision before I determine whether or not they can create a vision. I look for potential leaders who are willing to follow before they lead. I want to see if they can serve before they empower.

Do they add value to the vision given to them?
In other words, do they have the creativity to take a vision and make it better? Rather than blindly implementing the vision of another leader, potential leaders are able to improve upon the vision and make enhancements to it.

Do they show a high level of commitment to the vision?
After they buy into the vision, I want to know if they will pay the price to make the dream a reality. Potential leaders are willing to take responsibility for the vision.

Are they passionate about the vision?
A person can accept a vision and take steps toward its fulfillment, but I am searching for an added dimension of excitement and energy. I want a person with a contagious passion for the vision; someone with an infectious enjoyment who spreads the vision to others.

6. Do they show a willingness to take responsibility?

In my opinion, The Statue of Liberty should have a sister-statue—The Statue of Responsibility. People are quick to defend against infringements upon their freedom, but slow to take responsibility for their actions. Benjamin Franklin said, "I never knew a man that was good at making excuses who was good at anything else." Avoid choosing employees who are unwilling to take ownership or averse to responsibility. It's easier to go from failure to success than from excuses to success.

7. Do they finish the job?

The bookends of success are initiative and closure. If you cannot initiate, you cannot make things happen. If you cannot close, things that could happen never will.

Take notice of the projects you delegate to a potential leader. Do the jobs get completed 100%, or do they end up back at your desk demanding time and attention? The answer will tell you a lot about the leadership ability of the potential leader.

8. Are they emotionally strong?

No one can lead without being criticized or facing discouragement. A potential leader needs mental toughness. I don't want a mean leader, but I do want a tough-minded leader who confronts reality and pays the price of success.

9. Do they possess strong people skills?

Leaders with people skills will be more enjoyable to work with, and they will get more accomplished. Be wary of hiring a potential leader without friendliness, tact, or team spirit.

Observe whether the potential leader motivates or manipulates others. Motivation is moving people for mutual advantage, and it is a necessary leadership skill. Manipulation is moving people for personal advantage. Manipulation is always wrong and damaging to the health of teams and organizations.

Even without experience in a leadership position, potential leaders are already exerting influence in some capacity. Research their track record—both their achievements and their impact on the lives of those nearest them. If they can lead people without having a position, they'll do very well when they get one. If they can't lead people without a position, giving them a title will not help. The leader makes the position; the position doesn't make the leader.

10. Will they lead others with a servant's heart?

Servant-leaders never pursue a mission at the expense of their people. Rather, servant-leaders earn the loyalty and best efforts of their people by serving the interests and investing in the development of those they lead. A servant-leader leads to see others succeed.

Rabbi Kushner was right when he said, "The purpose of life is not to win.

The purpose of life is to grow and to share. When you come to look back on all that you've done in life, you will get more satisfaction from the pleasure you have brought into other people's lives than you will from the times that you outdid them and defeated them."

11. Can they make things happen?

Some people make things happen, and others wonder what happened.

Make sure a potential leader can produce.

Kansan poet Walt Mason gives expression to the value of a results-oriented producer in his poem, "The Man Who Delivers the Goods".

There is a man in the world who never gets turned down,

Wherever he chances to stray.

He gets the glad hand in the populous town,

Or out where the farmers make hay;

He is greeted with pleasure on deserts of sands,

And deep in the isles of the woods;

Wherever he goes there is a welcoming hand—

He's the man who delivers the goods.

One is too small a number to achieve greatness. To accomplish anything of significance, you must have the right people by your side. I trust these 11 questions will aid you as you pick potential leaders.

LESSON 11:

Keep Your Mind on the __________ __________.

The Pareto Principle (80/20)

- 80 percent of traffic jams occur on 20 percent of the roads.
- 80 percent of beer is consumed by 20 percent of drinkers.
- 80 percent of classroom participation comes from 20 percent of students.
- 80 percent of the time you wear 20 percent of your clothes.
- 80 percent of the profits come from only 20 percent of the customers.
- 80 percent of problems are generated by 20 percent of the employees.
- 80 percent of sales are generated by 20 percent of the sales people.
- 80 percent of all decisions can be made on 20 percent of the information.

What an eye opener this was for me. I realized it meant that the most productive 20 percent of my activities were sixteen times more productive than the remaining 80 percent. If I wanted to decrease the complexity of my life and increase my productivity, then I needed to focus on my top 20 percent. That day in the classroom I realized two things: (1) I was doing too many things, and (2) the things I was doing were often the wrong things. And that is a recipe for an ineffective life.

Five Decisions that Helped Me Become More Focused and Productive

1. I Determined Not to Know ______________

Some people believe that great leaders have all the answers. Not true. Successful leaders don't know everything. But they know people who do.

2. I Determined Not to Know Everything ____________

In any organization, problems should always be solved at the lowest level possible. If every problem must be shared with leaders first, then solutions take forever. Besides, the people on the front lines are usually the ones who provide the best solutions, whether it's on the production line, the battle line or the breadline.

3. I Determined to Let Someone ______________ Me

The decision to let others represent you requires much time and trust. It should not be given lightly. The person in whom you place that trust must earn it. However, once you reach that level of trust with people you work with, you will be freed up even more to remain focused on the main things that really matter.

4. I Determined to Stay with My Strengths and Not Work on My ____________

I read in the *Gallup Management Journal*, "The most revealing discovery [about the great leaders they studied] was that effective leaders have an acute sense of their own strengths and weakness. They know who they are—and who they are not…"

5. I Determined to Take Charge of What Took My _________ and __________

The final major step I took to help me keep my mind on the main thing was to take control my calendar. This was not easy for me. I enjoy helping people, and for the first few years of my career, other people often set my agenda and filled my calendar. Then one day I realized that I couldn't fulfill my purpose if I was forever fulfilling everyone else's.

The question is not: "Will my calendar be full?" but, "Who will fill my calendar?"

"Genius is the ability to reduce the complicated to the simple."

--C. W. Ceran

LESSON 12:

YOUR BIGGEST MISTAKE IS NOT ASKING WHAT ____________ YOU'RE MAKING

As I examined myself, I learned some things:

- I gave little thought to what might go wrong.
- I assumed that the "right way" would be mistake-free.
- I did not acknowledge mistakes I made to myself or others.
- I was not learning from my mistakes.
- I was not helping others by teaching lessons learned from my mistakes.

To get maximum attention … make a big ____________.

To cause maximum damage … fail to ____________ ________.

When it comes to success, the barrier is not the number of mistakes you make; it's the number of times you make the same mistake. If you want to want to learn to fail successfully and handle the mistakes you do make with maximum profit, then you need to do the following five things:

1. ______________ Your Own Mistakes and Weaknesses

You can't improve as a leader if you're too busy trying to pretend you are perfect.

2. Accept Mistakes as the Price of ______________

"The person interested in success has to learn to view failure as a healthy, inevitable part of the process of getting to the top."

--Joyce Brothers

3. Ask Yourself and Others, "What Are We ______________?"

The value of asking the question is that it causes everyone to stop and think. Many people can see what's obvious. Few can see what isn't there. Asking tough questions causes people to think differently. Not asking questions is to assume that a project is potentially perfect and that if it's handled with care there will be no problems. That simply isn't reality.

4. Give The People Around You Permission To ________ __________

Recently I saw a sign in a high-pressure sales office that read, "Do you like to travel? Do you want to meet new friends? Do you want to free up your future? All this can be yours if you make one more mistake."

Fear of making mistakes keeps many individuals from reaching their potential. Fear of being honest with leaders about the potential problems that a course of action might bring has hurt many teams. The best leaders invite the opinions of the people on their teams.

NOTES

LESSON 13:

DON'T MANAGE YOUR ______________— MANAGE YOUR ______________.

"Nothing else distinguishes effective executives as much as their tender loving care of time."

--Peter Drucker

________________________ is an oxymoron. You can no sooner manage time than lasso the wind. Time continues whether or not you manage it—and it comes to you in the same increments no matter how fast you think or act. The important thing is not managing your time but rather managing the tasks that fill your time.

"It is not enough to be busy. The question is, 'What are we busy about?'"

--Henry David Thoreau

How do you judge whether something is worthy of your time and attention?

For years I have used the following three-step formula to help me know the importance of a task so that I can manage myself effectively:

Step 1: Rate the task in terms of importance:

Critical = 5 points

Necessary = 4 points

Important = 3 points

Helpful = 2 points

Marginal = 1 point

Step 2: Decide the task's urgency regarding when it must be done:

This month = 5 points

Next month = 4 points

This quarter = 3 points

Next quarter = 2 points

End of year = 1 point

Step 3: Multiply the rate of importance times the rate of urgency. Example: 5 (critical) X 4 (next month) = 20.

I then judge when I should complete the task according to the following scale:

A = 16-25: Critical task to be finished by end of month

B = 9-15: Important task to be finished by end of quarter

C = 1-8: Low priority to be finished by end of year

As a reminder of the finite nature of time, I keep a card with me at all times with the words of writer and naturalist John Burroughs. It says,

> I still find each day too short…
>
> For all the thoughts I want to think,
>
> For all the walks I want to take,
>
> For all the books I want to read,
>
> For all the friends I want to see.

Manage the tasks of your life and you will make the most of your time.

LESSON 14:

KEEP ______________ TO KEEP ______________.

All great leaders invest themselves in a personal growth plan.

Suggestions for initiating your own personal growth plan:

1. Invest in Yourself ___________.

"You cannot lead others until you leader yourself first."

--Harry Truman

2. Be a Continual Learner.

"The moment you stop ___________ is the moment you stop _______________."

--Rick Warren

What kind of attitude do you have when it comes to learning? I've observed that people fall into one of three zones:

- The ___________ Zone: "I attempt to do what I haven't done before."
- The ___________ Zone: "I do what I already know I can do."
- The ___________ Zone: "I don't even do what I've done before."

To progress as a leader is to transition from being a person of answers to a person of lessons.

LESSON 15:

Leaders Distinguish Themselves During ____________ ______________.

Every leader faces tough times—and that's when leaders distinguish themselves and show who they really are. Leading others can be very difficult and can take great courage. Of course, it's not that way all of the time. About 95 percent of the decisions a CEO makes could be made by a reasonably intelligent high school graduate. What is often required is common sense. But CEOs don't get paid for those decisions; they get paid for the other 5 percent. Those are the tough calls.

How do you know when you're facing a tough call and need to be at your best as a leader? You'll know when the decision is marked by these two things:

1. The Tough Call Demands ______________.

Leaders have to be willing to do things others are unwilling to do. They have to put themselves on the line.

"The most striking thing about highly effective leaders is how little they have in common. What one swears by, another warns against. But one trait stands out: Effective leaders are willing to take a risk."

--Larry Osborne

2. The Tough Call Brings With It an ______________ ____________.

"All the significant battles are waged within self."

--Sheldon Koop

When I think about the difficult times I have faced as a leader, I recognize that every one of them began within me—not with others.

Chuck Swindoll writes, "Courage is not limited to the battlefield or the Indianapolis 500 or bravely catching a thief in your house. The real tests of courage are much quieter. They are the inner test, like remaining faithful when nobody's looking, like enduring pain when the room is empty, like standing alone when you're misunderstood."

Doing the right thing isn't always easy, but it is always necessary if a leader wants to maintain integrity and remain effective.

NOTES

LESSON 16:

People Quit ___________, Not Companies.

People coming in—join a ___________.

People going out—leave a ____________.

> *The Bob Principle:*
> *When Bob Has a Problem With ______________, Bob's Usually the Problem.*

Oscar Wilde said:

"Some people cause happiness ______________ they go.

Some people cause happiness ______________ they go."

Why Do People Quit?

Reason #1: People Quit People Who ______________ Them.

When leaders act superior and treat their people with disdain or even contempt, it spells disaster for any relationship.

Reason #2: People Quit People Who Are ___________________.

A survey conducted by Manchester Consulting indicates that trust in the workplace is on the decline. They discovered that the five quickest ways that leaders lost the trust of their people in the work place were:

1. Acting inconsistently in what they __________ and __________

2. Seeking ________________ gain above shared gain

3. ________________ information

4. ________________ or telling half-truths

5. Being ______________________

Reason #3: People Quit People Who Are _____________________.

When leaders are incompetent, they become a distraction to the team. They waste people's energy. They prevent people from keeping the main thing the main thing. They take the focus from the vision and values of the organization and place it on the behavior of the leader. If the people working for an incompetent leader have a high degree of skill, they will continually worry about the leader messing things up. If they don't have skill or experience, they won't know what to do. Either way, productivity declines, morale suffers and positive momentum becomes impossible.

Reason #4: People Quit People Who Are ____________________.

Exceptional leaders do two things well. They:

- Develop other _______________
- Work themselves _________ ______ ______ ___________

Insecure leaders do neither. Instead, they try to make themselves indispensable. They don't want to train their people to reach their potential and be more successful than they are. In fact, they don't want them to be able to succeed without their help. And any time someone who works for them rises up to too high a level, they see it as a threat.

Exceptional leaders aren't afraid to develop leaders better than themselves. They know such people will never quit; they will simply carry on their legacy.

LESSON 17:

________________ Is Not the Best Teacher.

We all begin our lives as empty notebooks. Every day we have an opportunity to record new experiences on our pages. With the turning of each page, we gain more knowledge and understanding. Ideally, as we progress our notebook becomes filled with notations and observations. The problem is that not all people make the best use of their notebooks.

Some people seem to leave the notebook closed most of their lives. They rarely jot anything down. Others fill their pages, but they never take the time to reflect on them and gain greater wisdom and understanding. But a few not only make a record of what they experience; they linger over it and ponder its meaning. They re-read what is written and reflect on it. Reflection turns experience into insight, so they not only live the experience, but learn from it. They understand that time is on their side if they use their notebook as a learning tool, not just as a calendar. They have come to understand a secret. Experience teaches nothing, but evaluated experience teaches everything.

If you want to gain from your experience—to become a wiser and more effective leader—there are some things about experience you need to know:

1. Our Attitude Toward ____________________ and

____________________ Experiences Determines Our Growth.

What we want and what we need are not always the same thing.

2. Lack of Experience Is ________________.

"The arrogance of the young is a direct result of not having known enough consequences. The turkey that every day greedily approaches the farmer who tosses him grain is not wrong. It is just that no one ever told him about Thanksgiving."

--Harry Golden

3. Experience Is Also ________________.

Lack of experience may be costly—but so is experience. It's a fact that you cannot gain experience without paying a price. The great American novelist Mark Twain once remarked, "I know a man who grabbed a cat by the tail and he learned 40 percent more about cats than the man who didn't."

4. Evaluated Experience Lifts a Person Above the ________________.

People who make it a regular practice to reflect on their experiences, evaluate what went wrong and right, and learn from them really are rare. But when you meet one, you know it.

NOTES

LESSON 18:

The Secret to a Good Meeting Is the Meeting ______________ the Meeting.

Olan Hendrix explained to me that meetings usually fail from the following two reasons:

1. The leader doesn't have a __________ agenda.

2. Other people in the meeting have their ___________ agendas.

The Value of Having The Meeting Before the Meeting

1. The Meeting Before the Meeting Helps Followers to __________

____

What people *see* is determined by where they *sit*. They naturally see things from their own perspective, not from anyone else's, including yours. As the leader, you need to help followers see things as you do. That requires time and intentionality.

2. The Meeting Before the Meeting Helps to Increase Your

____

Leadership is influence, nothing more, nothing less. How do you gain influence with people? You invest in them. How do you invest in them? It starts by giving them time.

3. The Meeting Before the Meeting Helps You Avoid Being

________________.

Advice for Effective Meetings:

- If you can't have the meeting before the meeting, don't have the meeting.
- If you do have the meeting before the meeting, but it's not a good meeting, don't have the meeting.
- If you have the meeting before the meeting and it's like the meeting you want to have, then have the meeting.

Good ________________ always costs less than good ______________.

NOTES

LESSON 19:

Be a ______________, Not Just a ______________.

My Early Misconceptions About Leadership:

1. I thought my leadership ______________ made me a leader.

2. I thought climbing the leadership ladder was __________ __________________ than connecting with people.

The Difference Between Climbers and Connectors

1. Climbers Think ___________—

   Connectors Think ____________

2. Climbers Focus on _______________—

   Connectors Focus on _________________

3. Climbers Value _________________—

   Connectors Value _________________

4. Climbers Seek _________________—

   Connectors Seek __________________

5. Climbers Build Their _________________—

   Connectors Build ___________________

If you climb without connecting, you may gain authority, but you won't have _______________ _________________.

If you connect well but possess little desire to climb, you may end up with many friends but not much authority to ____________________
________________________.

Climbing and connecting is not an either/or proposition; it's a both/and proposition. Great leaders understand how to do both well.

During the course of my career, I have changed from a climber to a connector, and I have no regrets. I can summarize the progress of my thinking in the following way. I went from:

I want to win.

to

I want to win, and you can too.

to

I want to win with you.

to

I want you to win, and I'll win too.

LESSON 20:

The Choices You Make, ___________ ___________.

I have identified three critical choices that govern how I conduct myself as a leader. At the end of the day, I believe these choices have made me a better leader.

Choosing Your Choices

Choice #1:
My Standards for Myself Will Be ________________ Than What Others Might Set For Me

I have made it my goal to set higher standards for myself than others might for me because I know that a sure way to fail as a leader is to do only the bare minimum. I have been studying leaders for more than forty years. It is my observation that great leaders are never satisfied with their current levels of performance. They are not only demanding of their people, but they also continually push themselves to reach their potential. Their expectations for themselves are always higher than any standards others might set for them.

"Excellence is the gradual result of always striving to do better."

--Pat Riley

Choice #2:
________________ People is More Important Than Making Them __________

When I finally came to the conclusion that it was more important for me to help people then to make them happy, I spent some time thinking about what that would mean for my leadership. After some reflection, here is what I determined:

Some people won't be happy when I . . .

- Uphold the ________________ of the organization before the ______________ of the people.
- Give some people more ____________________ than others.

- ________________ some people over others.
- Attempt to move them out of their ________________ ____________.
- Ask them to ________________ for the team.
- Choose the __________ picture over their ________________ picture.
- Make decisions they disagree with.

Choice #3:
My Focus Will Be on the ________________

A friend of mine recently said to me, "John, you have no rearview mirrors in your life. You live in the present." Although some might see that as criticism, I took it as a high compliment. I make a great effort to focus on what is right in front of me. For years I had a sign in my office that read, "Yesterday ended last night." It helped me to remain focused on the present.

Perhaps the wisest words I have ever read about choices were written by Portia Nelson in a piece entitled, "Autobiography in Five Short Chapters":

> *Chapter 1:* I walk down the street. There is a deep hole in the sidewalk. I fall in. I am lost—I am helpless. It isn't my fault. It takes forever to find a way out.
>
> *Chapter 2:* I walk down the same street. There is a deep hole in the sidewalk. I pretend I don't see it. I fall in again. I can't believe I am in the same place, but it isn't my fault. It still takes a long time to get out.
>
> *Chapter 3:* I walk down the same street. There is a deep hole in the sidewalk. I see it is there. I still fall in . . . it's a habit. My eyes are open. I know where I am. It is my fault. I get out immediately.
>
> *Chapter 4:* I walk down the same street. There is a deep hole in the sidewalk. I walk around it.
>
> *Chapter 5:* I walk down another street.

LESSON 21:

Influence Should Be ______________ but Never ________________.

The bigger leader you are, the more influence you will have. But influence has a purpose greater than that of bettering the life of the influencer. Boiled down to its essence, influence has value for three purposes:

1. Influence Exists to Speak Up for Those Who ________ Have Influence

Any leader who does not lift up the lives of other people is not fulfilling the highest leadership calling.

2. Influence Exists to Speak to Those Who ________ Have Influence

It is often difficult for anyone but a leader to get the ear of another leader.

3. Influence Exists to be Passed On to ____________

As my influence grew, people started asking me to extend my influence for them. Because my motivation as a leader was to help people, I gladly gave my influence to whoever asked for it—with no strings attached. Bad decision. I soon discovered that people were taking advantage of me. Here's what I learned:

- Some People Failed To Establish Their ______ ______________ Using My Influence
- Some People Took My Influence For ____________
- Some People Were Unable to Build the Organization by Passing on Influence to ____________
- Those Who Receive the Loan of My Influence Will Be ____________
- I Should Expect a ________ ________________ on My Loan

Recently I wrote something that expresses exactly how I feel about this issue. I call it, "My Loan Contract for Potential Leaders":

> I can give you a position of leadership.
>
> You must earn permission to lead.
>
> I can give you an opportunity to lead.
>
> You must make the best of that opportunity.
>
> I can set you up as a leader with potential.
>
> You must stay up by fulfilling your potential.
>
> I can get people to follow you today.
>
> You must get people to follow you tomorrow.
>
> My influence to you is a loan, not a gift.
>
> Express gratitude—Use it wisely.
>
> Give me a return on my investment.
>
> Give others a return on my investment.
>
> Give yourself a return on my investment.

LESSON 22:

For Everything You Gain, You ________ ______ Something.

"By avoiding risk, we really risk what is most important in life—reaching toward growth, our potential and a true contribution to a common goal."

--Max DePree

The real challenge is not giving up something in the beginning. There is typically little to give up then. The real challenge is moving forward when you must give up something significant.

One of my trusted mentors, Fred Smith, passed the following thoughts to me:

> Something in human nature tempts us to stay where we're comfortable. We try to find a plateau, a resting place, where we have comfortable stress and adequate finances. Where we have comfortable associations with people, without the intimidation of meeting new people and entering strange situations. Of course, all of us need to plateau for a time. We climb and then plateau for assimilation. But once we've assimilated what we've learned, we climb again. It's unfortunate when we've done our last climb. When we have made our last climb, we are old, whether forty or eighty.

Ten Tradeoffs Worth Making

1. Affirmation for ____________________

2. Security for ____________________

3. Financial Gain for ________________ ________________

4. Immediate Pleasure for ________________ ________________

5. Exploration for ____________

6. Quantity of Life for ________________ of Life

7. Acceptable for ________________

8. Addition for ________________

9. The First Half for the ________________ Half

10. Your work for God for a ________________ with God

Prayer at 60

Lord, as I grow older, I think I want to be known as . . .

Thoughtful, rather than gifted,

Loving, versus quick or bright,

Gentle, over being powerful,

A listener, more than a great communicator,

Available, rather than a hard worker,

Sacrificial, instead of successful,

Reliable, not famous,

Content, more than driven,

Self-controlled, rather than exciting,

Generous, instead of rich, and

Compassionate, more than competent.

I want to be a foot-washer.

Life won't let you progress without a price.

LESSON 23:

Those Who __________ the Journey With You Seldom ____________ with You.

Gaining Perspective

It has not been fun leaving some people behind on the journey. I miss many of them. I hope some of them miss me too. But that's how leadership works. The best you can hope to do is be prepared as people leave and to maintain the right perspective on it. I hope some of my mistakes will help you. Here are four that I made and had to correct:

1. I Waited For People I ____________ Have Waited For

2. I Felt ____________ When I Lost a Key Player

3. I Believed Important Players on My Team Couldn't Be ___________

4. I Had to Learn to Appreciate Those Who Were With Me Only a ____________ ____________

This lesson was one of the most difficult for me because I am a highly relational person. For years I assumed my closest teammates would be with me forever. It took me a few years but I finally discovered that…

- Not everyone *will* take the journey with you
- Not everyone *should* take the journey with you
- Not everyone *can* take the journey with you

Good leaders understand they are stewards. They must find the best people they can, giving them the opportunity to join in the journey, developing them and encouraging them to reach their potential. But they must also hold onto people lightly. Those who start with you seldom finish with you. And those who stay will be that much more special to you.

LESSON 24:

Few Leaders Are Successful Unless a Lot of People __________ __________ _____ _____.

When I look back at all the people who have help me along over the years, I realize they fall into two main groups: mentors and supporters. The mentors taught me, guided me, and many times took me under their wing. I am very grateful to them. Here's what's interesting about them:

1. Some Helped Me Who Never __________ __________.
2. Some Who Knew Me Never Knew They __________ __________.
3. Some Knew Me and __________ They Helped Me.

The mentors in my life have often reached down to me to draw me up to where they are. The supporters often take another role: they lift me up and make me better than I am on my own. As I think about all the different kinds of people who have taken and continue to take that role with me, I recognize that most of them fall into one of several categories. I'll list them because you may find it helpful for identifying the kinds of people who are also helping you:

Different Kinds of Supporters

- __________ __________—people who save me time.
- __________ __________—people who do things I am not gifted to do.
- __________ __________—people who add value to me and my team.
- __________ __________—people who solve problems and give me options.
- __________ __________—people who complete assignments with excellence.

- ______________ ______________—people who develop and raise up other leaders and producers.
- ______________ ______________—people who lead with the right attitude.
- __________ ______________—people who expand my thinking and my spirit.
- ______________ ______________—people who bring other people into my life who add value to me.
- ______________ ______________—people who encourage me in my faith walk.
- ______________ ______________—people who know my weaknesses, yet love me unconditionally.

The English word *thanks* comes from the same root word as *think*. Maybe if leaders were more "thinkful" about the contribution of others, they would be more "thankful" to them.

NOTES

____

____

____

____

____

____

____

____

LESSON 25:

YOU ONLY GET ________________ TO THE QUESTIONS YOU ________________.

Some people see questions as a sign of ignorance. Leaders see them as a sign of engagement, curiosity, and the desire to improve.

"He who asks is a fool for five minutes, but he who does not ask is a fool forever."
--Chinese Proverb

Author Brian Tracy said, "A major stimulant to creative thinking is focused questions. There is something about a well-worded question that often penetrates to the heart of the matter and triggers new ideas and insights." In general, the more thoughtful and precise the question, the better the answer.

"Quality questions create a quality life. Successful people ask better questions and as a result, they get better answers."
--Anthony Robbins

What questions you should ask and to whom they should be addressed depend on what work you do, where you are in your journey and how you want to grow. However, I can tell you this: Before you run out and interview a bunch of leaders, you need to ask *yourself* a few questions first. When you ask yourself the right questions, you get yourself on the right track as a leader. Then what you should ask and who you should ask will become clear. Here are ten questions you should initially, and then periodically, ask yourself:

1. **Am I investing in myself? – This is a Personal Growth question.**

2. **Am I genuinely interested in others? – This is a Motive question.**

3. **Am I doing what I love and loving what I do? – This is a Passion question.**

4. **Am I investing my time with the right people? – This is a Relationship question.**

5. **Am I staying in my strength zone? – This is an Effectiveness question.**

6. Am I taking others to a higher level? – This is a Mission question.

7. Am I taking care of today? – This is a success question.

8. Am I taking time to think? – This is a Strategic Leadership question.

9. Am I developing other leaders? – This is a Legacy question.

10. Am I pleasing God? – This is a Faith question.

The bottom line: If you don't ask questions—and ask the right ones—you won't get the answers you need to grow as a leader. And know this: if you are no longer asking questions as a leader, then you might as well buy a rocking chair, put it on your front porch, and call it a day, because you've already retired. To continue developing as a leader, ask the right questions of yourself and of the leaders around you who can help you grow.

NOTES

LESSON 26:

People Will Summarize Your Life in One Sentence—__________ ____ _______.

Someday you and I are going to die. And eventually our lives will be summarized in a single sentence. What do you want yours to be? Claire Booth Luce cleverly called this your "life-sentence." If you are intentional about creating your legacy, people at your funeral won't have to wonder what your life sentence was.

"Life is like a parachute jump, you've got to get it right the first time."

--Eleanor Roosevelt

What Will You Leave Behind?

1. __________ __________ the Legacy You Want To Leave Others.

"The average man does not know what to do with his life, yet wants another one which will last forever."

--Anatole France

I started thinking about my purpose in the late 1960s and it has continued to evolve. Here is how my sentence has changed over the years along with my thinking:

I want to be a great pastor.

I want to be a great communicator.

I want to be a great writer.

I want to be a great leader.

I want to add value to people.

I want to add value to leaders who multiply value to others.

2. _____________ _____________ the Legacy You Want To Leave

In his book *Training for Power and Leadership,* Grenville Kleiser writes:
Your life is like a book. The title page is your name, the preface your introductions to the world. The pages are a daily record of your efforts, trials, pleasures, discouragements, and achievements. Day by day your thoughts and acts are being inscribed in your book of life. Hour by hour, the record is being made that must stand for all time. Once the word 'finis' must be written, let it then be said of your book that it is a record of noble purpose, generous service, and work well-done.

3. _________________ Today the Value of a Good Legacy

Charles F. Kettering, inventor and one-time head of General Motors' research division, said, "The greatest thing this generation can do is lay a few stepping stones for the next generation."

To Determine Your Legacy Ask Three Questions

1. *What are my responsibilities?* (This helps identify what you should do.)

2. *What are my abilities?* (This helps identify what you can do.)

3. *What are my opportunities?* (This helps identify what you could do.)

There is a poem called "The Bridge Builder" that I have enjoyed for many years. It was written by Tennessee poet Will Allen Dromgoole, and describes what it means to create a legacy for those who follow us:

> An old man, going a lone highway,
>
> Came at the evening, cold and gray,
>
> To chasm, vast and deep and wide,
>
> Through which was flowing a sullen tide.
>
> The old man crossed in the twilight dim;

The sullen stream had no fears for him;
But he turned when safe on the other side
And built a bridge to span the tide.

"Old man," said a fellow pilgrim near,
"You are wasting strength with building here;
Your journey will end with the ending day;
You never again must pass this way;
You have crossed the chasm, deep and wide --
Why build you the bridge at the eventide?"

The builder lifted his old gray head:
"Good friend, in the path I have come," he said,
"There followeth after me today
A youth whose feet must pass this way.
This chasm that has been naught to me
To that fair-haired youth may a pit-fall be,
He, too, must cross in the twilight dim;
Good friend, I am building the bridge for him."

What kind of a bridge are you building for those who follow behind you? Are you making the most of your leadership—not just for yourself, not just for those who follow you today, but also for those who will follow you tomorrow? Knowing that someday people will summarize your life in one sentence is sobering. Picking it now is a way of saying "thank you" to God, life, family and others you will never meet.

"We should so live and labor in our time that what came to us as seed may go to the next generation as blossom; and what came to us as blossom may go to them as fruit. This is what we mean by progress."

--Henry Ward Beecher

NOTES

Leaving a Legitimate Leadership Legacy

John C. Maxwell

As I begin, I would be remiss not to mention the tremendous contribution of my friend Dick Biggs has made in shaping my thoughts on succession. Several of Dick's ideas are woven into this article.

A LEGACY OF FREEDOM

President Abraham Lincoln's leadership through the painful trial of Civil War saved the United States of America and ended the deplorable institution of slavery. In the war's aftermath, Lincoln faced the challenge of rebuilding the South without restoring its system of white supremacy. Balancing goodwill toward freed blacks and a conciliatory stance toward the former Confederate states, Lincoln appeared to have the perfect temperament to ease the South through a time of healing and into a period of prosperity and equality.

Abraham Lincoln's assassination plunged the fragile future of the South into uncertainty. His successor, President Andrew Johnson, continued policies of conciliation toward the Southern states, but he did not share Lincoln's regard for black Americans. By pardoning key leaders of the Confederacy and placing power back in the hands of state legislators in the South, Andrew Johnson reconstructed the South's oppressive system of white domination. Johnson's personal racism and inept leadership was responsible for stunting the progress of the civil rights movement and perpetuating injustice in the South for another 100 years.

Abraham Lincoln's tragic death followed by Andrew Johnson's deficiencies in rebuilding the South is a testament to the Law of Legacy:

"A Leader's Lasting Value is Measured by Succession."

Who knows how far or how quickly the USA may have progressed toward racial equality had Lincoln been able to pass the reins of the government to a like-minded leader?

LEAVING A LEGACY

A turning point in my leadership came when I began to understand the meaning of leaving a legacy. A catalyst for me was a simple statement from management expert, Peter Drucker:

"There is no success without a successor."

I had always wanted to create lasting value through my life and leadership, so I decided to take seriously the cultivation of successors. I resolved to produce leaders rather than attract followers, and it's one of the best decisions I've made in my leadership. In this lesson, I'd like to explore four aspects of shaping a legitimate leadership legacy:

1. Character
2. Choices
3. Conduct
4. Consequences

Character – Being and becoming a moral example

The two words most commonly linked to character are integrity and honesty. Integrity involves being true to oneself, while honesty means being truthful with others. Each involves being real not fake, genuine not artificial, transparent not deceitful.

You can't spell integrity without the word grit which is defined as "a firmness of mind," or "unyielding courage." It takes a great deal of courage or grit to be true to self. In the end, though, it's worth the effort because our legacies are going to be impacted greatly by our integrity or lack thereof.

Choices – Thinking clearly and making wise decisions

Careful decision-making requires a sense of right and wrong rooted in character. To make the right decisions consistently, we can't let external influence or peer pressure cause us to do something wrong when our internal conscience is telling us to do what is right. To violate conscience undermines our self-respect and shatters not only our moral authority, but our confidence as leaders.

We must also understand how pleasure and pain impact our choices. In short, if we enjoy temporary pleasure with a disregard for its harmful effects on us and other people, we're going to suffer long-term pain. Leadership demands sacrifices for the near-term to receive lasting benefits. The longer we wait to make sacrifices, the harder they become. Successful people make important decisions early in their life, then manage those decisions the rest of their lives.

Conduct – Doing the right things consistently well

Conduct is defined as "a mode of personal behavior." Only individuals can behave. The conduct of a company, government agency, sports team, or church is a reflection of the conduct of the individuals making up the organization.

To shape the conduct of the individuals who follow us, we must be able to hold them accountable for their behavior. But first, we must be held accountable ourselves. Author Chuck Swindoll says accountability is "a willingness to explain your actions." If our actions are indefensible, we'll be stripped of the real authority to exercise moral leadership. We must submit our behavior to the scrutiny of trusted advisors before dictating the conduct of those we lead.

As leaders, we set the tone for the conduct of the individuals in our organization. People do what people see. Conduct is learned through observation. As Dr. Michael Guido says, "The world pays more attention to your conduct than it does to your creed." As leaders, we teach what we know, but we reproduce who we are.

Consequences – Receiving the results of seeds that we sow

The success of my day is based on the seeds that I sow, not the harvest I reap. Too often, leaders bypass the process of sowing seeds in favor of shortcuts for results. Sadly, the end begins to justify the means, and principles are tossed out for more expedient behavior.

I've found submitting to the process of sowing the right seeds will meet with tremendous rewards—whether I see the fruits firsthand or not. Here are five reasons I believe in keeping my attention on sowing well rather than seeing instant results:

(1) The seeds I sow will determine the harvest I reap.

(2) There is no reaping unless I have been sowing.

(3) Sowers are committed to giving before receiving.

(4) Sowers enjoy giving more than receiving.

(5) Sowing daily into the lives of others will compound over time.

We spend our day either preparing or repairing. Preparing allows us to focus on today, while repairing forces us to clean up yesterday. Preparing invests for the future, repairing pays down past debts. Preparing increases efficiency, but repairing consumes precious time. Preparing increases confidence, while repairing breeds discouragement. Cherish each day to grow and develop, and avoid making mistakes which will return to haunt you. Remember: the secret of your success is determined by your daily agenda.

NOTES